TO THE MIDDLE
OF LOVE

OMAR SABBAGH

INDEPENDENT INNOVATIVE INTERNATIONAL

Published by Cinnamon Press
Meirion House
Tanygrisiau
Blaenau Ffestiniog
Gwynedd, LL41 3SU
www.cinnamonpress.com

Designed and typeset in Palatino by Cinnamon Press. Printed in Poland.

Original cover design by Adam Craig.

Cinnamon Press is represented in the UK by Inpress Ltd and in Wales by the Welsh Books Council.

Acknowledgements

With many thanks to the editors of the following journals or edited volumes, in which some of the poems (or earlier versions of such) have appeared: *Agenda, Agenda Online, CAPITALS, Peloton, Rusted Radishes, The Moth, The Warwick Review,* and *The Wolf.*

About the author

Omar Sabbagh is a widely published poet and critic. Two of his extant collections are: *My Only Ever Oedipal Complaint* and *The Square Root of Beirut* (Cinnamon Press, 2010/12); *To The Middle of Love* is his fourth collection. His Beirut novella, *Via Negativa: A Parable of Exile* was published by Liquorice Fish Books in March 2016. A Dubai sequel to the latter, *From Bourbon to Scotch,* is forthcoming in 2017. He has published essays on George Eliot, Ford Madox Ford, G.K. Chesterton, Robert Browning, Henry Miller, Lawrence Durrell, Joseph Conrad, and others; as well as many contemporary poets. He now teaches at the American University in Dubai (AUD).

Contents

What shall Cordelia speak? Love, and be silent.

William Shakespeare, *King Lear,* I, I, 60

for my parents, Mohamad and Maha Sabbagh

and for Faten

To The Middle of Love

That Chap Onan Again

In the vicinity of my birth, May was being a month in the scoundrel of time. All was maybe, mischief, scallywag. When I was born Death was criminal no more. He became a flute. And that dawn all extant violins were made the musts of a Midas-touch, so-many millions of them instantly petrified into gold. 'Never again, Beethoven,' was what the wind said outside the grey, concrete skirt of the Kensington hospital. 'Behold this plum hourglass: he is brine to every sea; he is more inkling than the inkling of water.' And the guts of that gale said, 'he is the beached world.' And the bowels within those guts, the hot maelstrom within that serpent of life said, 'he is what doesn't and will not cloy.' And the toenail of the snail which happened to be passing by bellowed: 'here is one slower than I, as shell to quicksand.' And the curs' excrement on the stone pavement said, in smells, in smells, 'here is an imbecile without an anus, lucky he, lucky he.' And the marooned baby lying next to him whispered to the susurrus, 'my neighbor is common sense, like the beard of a lion.' And the one parrot in heaven shouted, 'I have no more colors, the canary-yellow and the pepper-red are become shibboleths.' And there was in purgatory at that birthing moment a giraffe which did sodomize a monkey which rendered fellatio to an ant which was dealing heroin to bacteria, which said, 'hail, hail, hail-fellow-well-met.' And the moon in a mood said, 'the night is in his eyes, and I surrender.' And God was articulate as a minus number, clambering towards its square root. And the universe was noise for a moment, becoming sound and sauce for the big ears of a nightingale on its witty adventures. And Keats wrote about a cuckoo instead, as the ducks gangbanged. And cadence was a foe to cadence, a moan within a moan which unmanned that moan in a way that made that moan unlike a moan, which is, by its verynature, a thing unmanned. Let the Kleenex gather the spilling of this circus, let the tissue marry the hand and conceive: tissue of its tissue. Let what bates the wolf mar his jaws, his dentist late as a star.

As he loses his mind

Wand-stroke
past wand-stroke,

        the air

around me quilts

        the air

with mercurial pleats,

elfish idioms, a race,
a race
of suspicions…

I've invented a language for Onan.

One whose words
ripple like fingers
a-doll the piano-bones
of one's conceit,

black, white,
black, white
and all that's
        in-between…

So here's a lingo
for Onan,

a fierce pidgin
that tries,

tries to unlock
a smidgeon
of sense,

but fails
in the winding of that opening
of halest

religion.

Onan is dying
because Onan is living.
His crime

was always forgiving.

Aida

A pair of black stilettos there, stalking the ground:

A taut, kiss-poised
Heel-shouldered stillness
Pertly breaks into light,

And she's clearly un-hunted, hurrying through this
Rare,
Bear-round
Body of gladness

Within the all-quiet
Of his barely-met,
So badly-set,

Wide and alone...

So: this
Sweet-daft honey of bawling fun, this
Stinging
        gadfly pinging
                against
This pelt,

A slow, a very
Arching and slow
Breach-far beckoning
Forest and reckoning
Of yeast-hued ferns

Speaking,
           petite in ochre—
                    all this
Moan-tanned business
Of pin-sad, tone-mad pidgin,

And slim-soles, and well-mannered bone-patterns…

The sight of her nut-brown skin
Drapes the rose-blue night
                close and tight
With a smithy of love and her
Wet,
Her wet proud epigones…

I Must Think Myself Of Little Worth

Though the gusto of my brave designs
Has me hurling stomping titans line by line—
I think myself of little worth. The grand quiet
Slotted here, my grace amid a world's ruckus-riot,

Needs must be the Sire of a different child.
And if they speak psychology, of hard denial,
In the end they may not err, at the plump, final
Hour—the lonely one, stranded in the wild…

I'm no savage, even to myself. I sign my
Breast like everyone else, toting my truth.
So at daybreak here, my question's use
Goes simply as a bargain with the highest high-

est noose: where were You when I didn't know
Why the world was beating me like trampled snow?

The Bad Minuet

Blue Note Café, Hamra, Beirut, Lebanon
For C

Critters spray dross across the dance-floor
As though it was a critical step, a door
From garbage to what came after, before.
Cretins ape with ambition, a mimesis for
The poor in spirit—their innards: sea-less piers,
A drop onto waves of old-aged wood. Fear's
Boutique. Unworn dresses in raining tears.
Unworn women. *O the years, the years!*

     ***

If I kiss her spine in memory, her bare
Neck, the white of her, the white of her,
Her quid pro quo, her: *daring and near*—
If so—in that long ago—I become livid fire,
Plum, mauve, deep and purple with scaling care.
Not a day goes by I don't think of that far
Night, tripping on lightning, a speeding hare
In my head, my dizzy mind turned fare

                for the future.

La Veuve

Prague, Hamra, Beirut, Lebanon
For Pamela

She wears black, a widow busy with her widowhood.
The drapery's patrician in its pattern and flow.
Eyeing her, I seem to tug at her: like a poem to its sounds,
A levying of tax and vengeance here: against all blondes
And the sillier kinds of seeming behind Venetian blinds.

She wears black, like a lewd rhapsody against snow—
A jeremiad and a passion and a paradox in its folds;
Something wailing, Pre-Raphaelite, warming, saucing the cold
And raw, the fillet-leanness of a man, small as his mould,
Here within the essays and seeds of a fetal nation: *Egypt, I am old!*

She wears black, like sorrow, a tall minaret to her self,
And she's the dire, expressive lack of the sky-loud muezzin.
And in death she'll be more to me than my father's Liban
And the joyful grief of a mourning son, rent from Golgotha to hell.

'Dark Wood'

For Jeni Oppenheimer

The idea behind her skirt was metaphysical.
A sex caressed more by sun than by the maul,
The mundane maul.
                    It was unanswerable.

Logic became a living, fretting bird in its wake.
It was arch, necessary, absent to itself
As any winning joke
Told and told again from health to health.

There was a thimble-small element of fear as well.
But I won't go into that, that 'dark wood', that middle.

When We Meet

For Faten

When we meet, it'll be a shriek by freedom.
And all the domes and cupolas of Jerusalem will be
Less round than she, my love and me.

A bird now chirps on my balcony.
A pink and brown wood-pigeon, I assume...
I've met a different Oryx here, a focus and a zoom

Into the grim passing territory
Of whom I used to be. And she may be
The final curtain to close my house of rooms.

More Serious Lines (For More Serious Times)

Dubai, for Faten

A tether, ribbed by twining fibers, comes apart,
The nerves brighten like sparks, cleverer
By half. And they fashion a chaos that's dear
As you—neophyte, newcomer… My heart
Is old as a child's heart. The red, the undeterred
Red, is so red it vanishes to the null-point
Of a pin. My syllables are like straining ligaments,
And I'm unsure, unsure: if / which way to bend…

If I knew there was a way to rend time, wreck
The past's humdrum conundrum, a bottleneck,
I would. But this green hourglass, tossed, buoyed by
The burly weeping gushes of a great blue sea,
Is no message, no missive to You… *And yet the lies*
And the ultimatums of the lies: the full stock,
I mean—*well*, as the bricks, toppling, descend
From my torn and breaking mansion, I realize

The place of you may be a salve, slaking there,
To mend, sew, and suture the wounds of Care.

Golden

For Mohamad and Maha Sabbagh, best of parents

And shocked from the mouths of your children
Hale thanks for the hearthside you forged, make
Again and again….
                Our lives tomb-less-ly shake
With the spree of our gladness—*and no rum coffin*
Will ever thieve that load / rob us our burden,

Your wordy treasures, and all your deeds, and
The bounty of your shameless love. No wake
Will ever sway against the trays you made—*yourselves*
For us—no lime or lemon will ever mar our love…

Be at peace, then…

            Face your four burly limbs—two girls,
Two boys; they grace the world like number, uncoiled
Springs: readied to unfurl, again and again:

                    but no nail's to pin
Or sadly sully brown with brown—

                  we're the masts / the sails
                  you've purred
                  to live….

Our ship goes named—like Latin on a flower.

A Wish At The End Of Autumn

The ash-brown, ash-thyme curlicue
Of a winding-
Dying leaf, speaks,

A brittle utterance of passing
Unction. Dire duck-
Colored leaf, resume,

Take up the property of your room
In this house of roused music...

The phoenix
The lore of which
Is crud-ridden

Is a student
Here, where poor is rich,
Crossed suffering, tock: ticked

The Cedar Never Dies

My country, my love,
Let me speak to you now in a foreign tongue,
Quipping against the flaming madness
Now begun,
The language in which I body my caress,
My missive in Dove…

My country, my love,
Tell them the Cedar never dies, and She will rise,
A Phoenix without the need
Of ligaments, ligaments or knees…
A sour privilege to be, and concede
Against the flung velvet of a glove

The asking seed of daring gauntlets, my
Country, my love:
Let these words meet, though in a different tongue,
Your flesh of green, your never-ending rungs.

Her Kindness

For Fiona

You say to yourself, in many different tongues,
I will be better, I will be better in the morning.
And you may scour and scurry your mind for
The place where kindness is a revolving door,
An entrance, a welcoming, an inception... More.
And you will find it in the mother of things
You may have written, and you will find it in
A woman whose heart ushers *a sky* to begin—

The summit of honey, say, and the precipice,
The hive / the guiding eyes of one: so generous...

Mother Of All Things Quiet

For Maha Faris Sabbagh, on her birthday

Mother of all things domed and quiet, listen...
The flex and bend of fads / of mad contortions
Has been my holiday, sacred, though ribbed
With wrongs. A tad too dud, I've been more the bib
Than the well-combed child stomaching his food,
His little paunch of magic, small and round and rude.

I've been more the tangle / the virulent twine
Of fibrous tissue, more of laughing chaos than
The closed home of the erstwhile muscle. I've been
All I could be in a time of rage-wild contagion
And troubles. I miss the cuddle of your wand.
I miss the reigning-fact of being more than I am.

I miss the wise patterning of your hands
And how, like a grand idea turned obsolete,
You understand everything: and all was neat
And clear, whirling crystals of a taut dancing
Where no Bacchanal insisted—just simple feet
Moving and stirring a skeleton of bones into song.

A Dear Friend Grieves

For Patricia McCarthy

Foursquare,
The muscles taut with her loving,
There was nothing
Trojan or double or troubling
About the foursquare mare…

And there was no horsing around
In that companionship: a bond,
A deep and edgeless bond…
Ripped now with sorrow,
Ripped now

By wailing tears, riven, she rows
Whitewaters without sound.

A Moustachioed Priesthood In The Bar

Ferdinand, Hamra, Beirut, Lebanon. For Shady Jaber

The wooden counter in the bar's a *prie-Dieu* for
Lost causes, toppling, tumbling bellies, fumbles
At the sly door of Womanhood, the still / unstill
Windowsill.
                  And the blues' drapery's absurdity, their
                  quick, queer
Mores, speak volumes to the groans
And hard hopes of this
Stood, priestly Dali...
                  Ease says the face, won suaveness.
Any taut madness in his dreams is a fenced madness.
There is trust here:
                  As though there was no danger, nor a single risk
                  Within the strict cuss of this Lebanese sickness—
                  To undress and undress the dressed, to tear at the
      tears
                  Of the worse off—and only money there to care for.

Shady mans the scars, and the worn wounds entering the bar.

Keeping On Keeping On Going

And I am the Sultan of weeping,
The authority of hurt's a plum in my keeping,
And I am the Sultan of weeping...

Cuts cry in me, feats of vast-slow feeling,
While no suture arrives, kneeling
Upon an in-wending wind... The wedding

Of spirit and matter's an affair
Of dogs-bidding, dogs-bedding, digging
For some final theodicy of care...

I keep on keep on going.
There's something sweetly-neat in
Sewing the welts within in-

To the fabric of the world, the world's white skin.
And if I'm sore and rash, and have been
A small, sordid, an undressed wound

Upon the hills and mounds of my kin—
Let me remind them of the well-met mountain
We climb, as ever, and all, at the end.

Muhajabeen

Yas, Olympia

I won't tell what girds, what taxes her.
I won't opt for the obvious surd —

The obvious, telltale surd

Much like a moon-cussed straitjacket,
The lame and awry, the fat
Of a leper
Of a predicate.

Let the copula bellow its own shrill fame,
As sole shark to a globular sea.

And let the brine be what bite, what blood, what
Cold, what dark's writ and opted for me —

Chess to checkers, baroque to matt
As it ever was…

Let the walking illusions pray
Their heavy musk,
Like a mother who feels her wrongs…

Like the mother beveled before
The first apple or
The first mummer
In mammary,

And I more and more
And I descried and I discerned

Echoic from the blend
With high and mortal intents

And whatever else is meant
By sots in the café,
By hearts for sale, by hearts for rent.

No.
I won't tell what girds, what taxes her.

Another Icarus

For Nadim Fakhoury, on his 8th birthday

Dear boy,
I want to speak to you now in the gummy slang of youth,

Where the waving wand still sparkles, still rules,
Where the tongue leaps beyond the mouth,

And metaphor's hip hops remain
A babbling and a ploy

Like light through a windowpane, truths,
Dear boy,

Still raining in
The labile country

Of your undefiled
Innocence.

Lush and green, sweetly
Billowing, and immense…

Dear boy,
Beware the slimness of your entrance

To the world of ideal stillness and sterling sense:
The quick and nude wits of us

Who scrape—*but too close, too fast*—
By the sun, by the sun's disgust

For the white heat of the dawn-hued musk
Emitted from the wide-eyed Icarus

In the both of us...
Those gifts of God's swift touch,

Dear boy,
Are like crisp cool water for us

In whose minds God entrusts
All that God must

Between sap and dust...
So keep to the wide canyon of the sky,

Dear boy,
But be rid of the smirk and grin

And the many foils
Of those sham ambitions

Finning at the abyss
To sully and rend and spoil—

The high kinless-ness
Of the unearned Guinea, the vacant lust,

Dear boy,
Dear boy...

Fathers

For the Haddad Family

I know my father. They know theirs.
And between the winking of an eye
Each father declares
Steel missions of rubble and aching,
Feeling the ticks of rising Time,
Sun-splendor, sovereign rhyme —

Father, to you, I commend this song
Of words beyond the briefs of sundry signs…

And your sleeping agony's mine because
The forestry of your lap once greenly was
My body's prop, my small, my final cause —

Arenas of four burly oaken doors
Striding into the future

And that life that farther life adores.

On His 75th Birthday

For my beloved father, Mohamad Sabbagh

The world is cold, father: this fruit that stings, left-over, unsold…
And though you're first among equals, the prime of parents,
You're younger than the ground, and clay's first red: and I am old

As the first syllable of the first grammar of this grinding world…
You were ever the merit of the slow and manly sun, my hot dissent
Against a world of cold, father: cruel acids in a market, unsold…

I don't think the air around holds much fear for us, bold
Warriors, fighters for sense, needed, apt, and love-immense —
You're younger than the ground, father, and like clay, I am old…

All roads lead to Rome, a homely tale, a tale well-told — though,
Until we pass, shocked by black, we'll never know what was meant
By all this cold, never know the fruit that's bitter from the sweet.

Your role's been *pater* to a point-too-moot, and shelter from the cold
In a market-space where these fears have aged, my body's rent
By the ground itself, my Oryx-eyes stung by sighs, and I am old…

Father — that pear I stole in the garden, fruit hammering my soul,
Well, in the workshop of the world, you were always *First Artisan*,
Old man, young man, tilling the soil, digging — your tools
Were your hands, the grub of the ground; father of clay: I am sold.

Byblos

For Zoha

The waves come lashing, harsh and crashing,
And green turns the color of my heart.

The sun's white's a sinner upon this sea;
The leveling of all forgiveness enters me,

And the principal of this cursive art's
A bay-window, gardening the eye, and song

Like the robes of blinding light bedecking
This body of bliss, seated, at ease, a king

With the gift of friendship, by and bye;
The world's a neat space here. It cannot lie.

Music Of The World's Defeat

That we are simply nothing within
Each moment; that we are spread thin
By the light wisp of time's wrap and skin—

That we are cusps without feet, fleeting;
That *there is no* measure or meeting
Between the notes, no cause, no ceiling,

Close-cropped, or cornice of feeling
Which, like a black glove, gives meaning
To the bareness and desert of plumed hands,

Pink palms mixed with the color of sand
And sallow-and-tawny-tanned
Rock; that we've no gold on command—

That we're momentary, slipshod and weak—
Is a very library to me; tells me, in neat
Poised poetry: that, *at the least*,

I live in a world of thieves and cheats,
Broken numbers, brittle, rubber-meats—
That I live alone, and only

For the world's defeat.

The World's Reject

This is an old adage
The people, in thick massage,
Have branded me.

To this day,
My spine tingles with that sorry spree
Of clean and clear camaraderie.

I've mauled and mauled
The only God I know.
And He was tall, of course, and I

Below; under the footprint
That was god-sent,
That was rich and opulent

With a wisdom I've yet to build
Inside my tent
Of life. The makeshift gills

I've breathed with, this
Past and trussed and cursed
Briny kiss with nothingness,

A decade, but more,
Are slits, for all their
Insipidness, forced,

I've come to test,
To test and to adore.
But the sea was never this.

The world's reject is
Dismissed by cause
Of unknown laws

He travels with, like
Foreign friends. He hikes
With them everywhere,

Clueless of their tongue.
He's traveled the globe, thus,
And won, and won

Nothing but the inch before
The inch before
The merely next implicit rung

On a ladder
He'll not contemplate
Anymore.

He's tired, and fate
Can shove itself in the grate
Of its own fat fire…

But then of course
Fate was ever
At home inside that burning Morse.

Sonnets After Augustine's *Confessions*

1. Hearsay

After Chapter 1 of Augustine's Confessions

I start with hearsay: how I entered a pact
With the past, heaving like an oath towards fact.
I knew my childhood through the dim regard
I had of others, later, when old-age wore this bard.
I'd no inkling for Homeric Greek. I loved my Latin.
Words—after cries and wails and screams, grins
And belches—I learnt by use, in time—a mime—as well…
A philosopher, I believe, would descry—*pell-mell*—
How one learns to speak and know and meet the meat
Of others—by 'language-games,' and fission-fleets
Of them. But that was well beyond a millennium
Later: by then, I was safe and snug in your dominium,
Lord… I was beatified, dubbed a Saint: prose to meter;
And this verse serves to limn my first and deepest winter.

2. A Sex Espied

After Chapter 2 of Augustine's Confessions

At sixteen, you find me idle, school-bereft.
Father takes me to the baths, espies my sex,
And is delighted at the nearing prospect
Of grandkids. He goes out of his way
To collect the funds to send me, spritely, gay,
Onto Carthage. Meanwhile, Mother is
God's reflector, shame in my shamelessness…
In this eon of life, I loved only to reign as rake;
Peer pressure abounds, a kind of vice in trust…
What is evil, but wrong done for its own sake—
Not, thus, from Need? I see myself still, nip, take
That gorgeous extant, God's instance: a ripe pear…
None think they wrong wholly, or, in total, err!
I'm the exception. Inside rapine, I found Care.

3. A Dent In The Light

After Chapter 3 of Augustine's Confessions

Little later in life the flesh flew fey and wild, a Gnosis;
I gorged myself, my very meat: a fluent waylaid course...
Just so, against Plato, I rued a playful muse, a mad bourse
Aimed, like trickery, to thread me through, spent, hoarse
At the viscera's use—the tragic lay of some pagan wretch...
My mother, of course, knew better, bigger, more.
She knew that wrong was a whore without a stitch
Of true or gladsome garb—just flesh, flesh and absence...
Still, my peers harrowed me, the urge of naked sense
In parity with spirit—as if there were living fish
Whose sea was deep, but sky-denied: high culture into kitsch...
They would twist the negative, the bleak, the black: to a fetish.
Little did I know: I, a loon, facing the mighty fundament
Of Good; Evil: a mere gap in the light, light askew, a dent.

Milton's Satan And I

Like him: I won't, I won't ever give in.
Time and Space will find me ever the same:

A fish, say—slit with pity and gills—but found
Out of water; neither water: gem-like and pellucid,
Nor the dizzy scallywag of the saltier kind;

Never, then, to pursue and then to bevel in
The close strum of a home, a reigning warmth—
But to remain—a wailing extant,
                                    without a Name
Or whatever manly thing stands for Hope.

Better to rule in hell than to serve the Pope
Or his comrades, be they Jews or Muslims,
Or Buddhists reeling like they're doped
Beyond the bordered self's glad hallo—

That self: I am—it's most definite—that self I quote,
Deriving my eyes from only my own Titanic coat,
Which straps me like a madman against the cold.

Stubborn, fixed, sure, proud, bawdy and bold,
I'm more like Milton's bad-boy, flung into a hole

Where I won't, I won't ever give in: my role
To be a big and painful pin in the side of those
Of better mould.

When The Martyrs Go

After Mahmoud Darwish

When the martyrs bend low to the dark chamber of sleep, I waken
and guard them from the kitsch professions
of the moneyed mourners.

I tell them: rise on a country of wool and willow,
dreams and streams.

I commend them to the keep, saved from the horror
of the unspeakable event,
and from the cup of blood brimming over with slaughter

And I write their lives in verse
to become immortal as them:
aren't we all martyrs, waiting patient in the hearse
of the living?

And I whisper: leave one wall steady
for the laundry lines, give us moonlight
so we may sing in tandem and tow.

I will drape your names with the backwash of your parting desires,
so go in peace, and peacefully lie
on the boughs of the sour-vine tree.

I guard your sharpest desires
from the softening of the gods
and the sharper bones of the prophets' tome.

Be the voice of those who have no voice
when you pass over us tonight, for we are the sump of your sacrifice
and choice...
                    however choiceless...

I tell you: rise on a motherland that was suckled
then whisked away on a galloping mare.

I whisper: my friends, you'll never be like us...
who live and lose, speaking amidst unspeakable gusts.

The Bird In The Tree

It was as if
         a film
               of surreal gloss
Circled the triangle
Of that figure—so black
It was purple;
         a painter's wicked slash
Of coal-grey across
         the black breast,
         a heart-thick
         diagonal,
The only sign of life, or of interest
In the same…

         The bird in the tree
         seemed lost,
Foundering, a perched dream through a crack
In the seam
         of the workaday reality.
         Was it silly of me to see

That weird
White-lined aura that freed
The bird from the custom of the picture?

As though some wraith, a slim cure,
Some rapier
Of sublime pencil
Had tracked its shape
To a strangely-mental
Completion—

it was no more bird,
no more simple
Avatar / epigone
of the reptile,

But a voice in black in the white world,
But a voice on the eye that the eye heard.

The Reality Of It

Has been a flying dinosaur's wing
Found in the muddy earth, a deep shilling
From the gold standard of yesterday.

Has been the privacy of a well-lit play,
The boards treaded by walking flames,
Ratty pigeons in the scale of things.

Has been the door through which a sire
Goes wedded to a duck, makes a liar
Out of love, makes a liar a liar.

Has been the whole of Africa in
The sweaty palm of an Indian,
Some such transient confusion.

Has been too many clocks to fit
The wall of a reading room, the sins
Of learning, deep, like a covert kit

In a battle a-rage over all but
That all which ends and begins
Eternally as friendship.

Has been the torture at the spine
Of a bacterium, or a viral portent in
A Eucharist of wreckage, half-spelt signs.

Has been the major tenor of a life
In which no vehicle is quite
Good enough

To make sense of this bloody mire
In which blood-cells go cheap and for hire—
A cock-up, overall, too much wrong for the lair

Of one beholden man, beholding
The same—and the thick, grisly maze of fear
Through which he scurries: golden / unfolding.

Whiskey At The Turrets

It takes little time for a man to know
The flippant murderers that graft
Like growths inside of him.

In his kingdom, in his ransomed realm,
A dark mythos spreads itself
Like fingers in a pattern

Of hands, waving to survive.
He does all he can,
He does all he can to man the sail

That may take him to that blind-spot
On the map, peopled and plowed
By these thrilled and shining nations,

And the different idioms spelt,
Countries and tongues and
A sum of dominions that speak

To the pidgin of the raw pink of welts.
Imagine his wounds knelt
In forlorn vigil,

The spilling flesh, the bowels
Of a fish, gutted-open,
But still shimmering

With midget-pulse, a life;
This, my fist of whiskey's vibrant,
Vital, yes, vital

And alive
At the turrets,
The sole friend ready, able,

To fling his mane of arrows
Smelt to an oaken gold
At enemies approaching…

Within his soul, within his glassy soul,
My stony friend,
My friend,

An ancient magic grows old.

The Salvaging

Yas, Kensington, London

Imagine a fisherman with an infinite net:
His little grey boat, posed, like an infinite bet
Against a sea's wide slurs, her echolalia…

Out of all the fey rhapsodies and masks
The uncaught fish finds his focus, his home
And the spindly fern-pattern before his
Spindly heart, like ribs like fast

                  empty wishes,
His slim and slippery task:
              to be a fish was always daft…

But the bone-thin fisherman,
                bereft the kisses
Of some mastered art, turns riled and vicious
And stark,
      a poverty facing the patent riches
Of the glittering, safe, mislaid, dispersed

Fish among fishes…

The Robes Of Evening

Dubai

Down-wending, draping lavender in white,
This evening's sky's a fist without a fight.

Or perhaps the inverse:
                            with bullies to the right
And bullies to the left, the pen's palm crunches
Though un-collapsible otherwise....
                            Hint-hunches
In the same old shadow-play,
Shadow, though, doubled, double-bright...

Avenues seem walking instead of walked:
                            the lame punches
Dapper, plosive as a folded napkin.
                            As taut.

In the hoary air of the mad gull-gossip, dinner descends
To robe my hunger.
                    Passing day's

Resumed in a solution of knuckled whiskey...

The gowned sun, the late, dray-like sun
Grows bereft. Lost rum. Loss: in sum.

A Vast Pyramid Of Papers

I'd need a tribe of slaves to grade these papers.
They pile high, a vast pyramid of heartless stone.
And no one knows what it's like to be owned
By boorish duty, by pigs of wonky slurs
In the English tongue, slim passengers or
Failing marrow: unhoused in a licit bone.
The clock ticks, and the weekend's like Autumn,
The leaves of my mind grow brittle and brown.

The Concrete Monster

Somehow, it shot up, its many-barreled layers of grey
Slate-colored sheets, decking against what used to be
Air. To the pin-drop of night-unction, you can hear
Them maneuvering against the manumission of air.

I'm monstered by sallying noise, as though no care
Were taken for silence, a piece of happy poverty,
However hidden, latent, however buried and weird—
As though steeds were caught astride themselves, the mares

They should be mating, chest-hurt, wounded in the bare
Womanhood—while the males of concrete disturb
All that was empty but somehow complete. Words
Fail to shadow and veil what shadows and veils.

Under The Desert-Sun

Dubai

Woodpigeons
                    chirp and holler

And here's me, I hear
                    the echoes
Of beastly human voices, saying,

Among things
                    of an-other

Different wounding nature:

                    Please
                    infer,
                                        infer

From us the matt pathos
That you are,
Built of bones like the rest of us,

But pulsing
With the stubborn stick /

With the outright cuss
Of blood-rills
                    like stones

In hard queues of other,
                    bigger stones…

*

I've tried to barter with the birds in styled
Rhetoric, a sophist-to-gloss-and-win,
As ever, as ever…

But loss is unique;
    she has no twin…

*

And death, too, the birds opine.
      Death, whose
Sign's a hammer to flatten all words, Muse

Or no muse…

   Does that mean
   I'm the nail:
I ask my friends, brown and beige and reptilian?

They cluck their tongues. They warble,
      they warble—

The unfortunate son
    whose curse is noble,

This hobbling child, a moth on carpet, under the desert-sun.

Idling

Four days now, a midget in the shade,
The tree I lie beneath, idling, busy
With his parable
Which limns a lay of wry dispersal
About the days' dock, and the dock of day...

Four days now, homunculus
Praying to his rummy south
And waiting for the trigger
Of the telltale bell
Which may clang the call to work. Work...

The week has been a bitter splay
Of crumbs. No bready mouth
Was ever munched by such a lazy lout.
And on the fifth day, too, he did naught...

The sixth day came to be
A bonanza to cup and cradle
All his hopes. And the seventh was
To be the idle reminder

That idling was never less kind.
That idling was ever the unluckiest sign
Of too much kindness
Becoming kinder...

To The Middle Of Love

Seamus Heaney, Rest In Peace

Though you never knew me, more than a knowing nod
From the TV; though you near-wept as you read
About your father, a blackbird, and more, much more;
And though you were the festival in your finite life,

Now stroll, beyond all wanderings, naming no error
In those halcyon gardens where all are careless with their
Care; *now amble*, don't hesitate: there the poems are quiet
As fires without denizens or hasty feelings for the air
In which they billow, yellow, red, blue as an apple-core…

No. You are not dead, spent, gone. You are

What the birds sing at hallowed morning, knowing the more
In store, knowing what good speed, what loaded dares
Are meant by the passing of a bard to the middle
Of everything. To the middle of love. That's all.

The Source, At The Last, Of His Self-Confidence

For Maha Faris Sabbagh

They will assume. But it's not the trappings
Of the mandarin that speak me. That tower,
I know, is very thin – close always to toppling…

Rather, at the lasting source of his belly's
Water, you'll find in the dare of your belief
The man goes thieved by a deep humility.

Not before you, perhaps, or you, or you,
But as though sprung from the beef
And blue of a mother, the bind, the cue

To be earth-bound like only the very few…
She leant him a sureness; it accrues, the more
And more, the more you find in him the flaw

Of that mute presence-of-mind that draws
On swift mathematics: much as the adoration
Of She whose gambit was ever completion.

The androgynous seer, to be found waiting
In Plato and Jung, speaks my language
Of dues owed to a perfect road: a silly rage

Where the man or woman yet come to know
That weakness at the source of the carapace
Is strength, if recognized, if gathered in the bliss

Of a silence we also know – man, woman –
The sufferance in burly spite, locked in a pain
Where no key's apt, to twist / to dub your name…

At the last, understood, they may well ask:
'But how can you live like that?' A rasp
In answer, I may say, 'Yes, and that itself was

Half the task which set myself, bound me in the kiss
Of fate and survival.' I lived by the atom, and this
Is now my end of earth: and a great, grand separation.

A Lamentation At Dawn, Dubai

For C

The light outside the window's
A finger of sailing-blue.
The moon, by chance, is svelte
And shines, a milky child,
Unnamed, without curfew.

The voices of the night
Have stirred in me again...
I wake to a world,
I wake to a world
Shaped in deep-crowned purple,

A sepulcher
Of all I am and was,
Of me, of her,
The Cross
Of our dissent.

The way things went, torn, sundered, rent:
Our skin: so weeping-ly-brittle!
All that was / and all that was
Like bitter salt, flourished
And prospered—

Scales of a shimmying fish
In fresh, clean water,
Glittering upwards to her finish
At the top of the hill;
Our swimming was tide-less,

You see, strange, and strangely-quiet—
And utterly surreal...
Our muffled mouths
Were like veiled stars, veiled
In a slow sky in a slow night,

The time it took to reach us,
The light, I mean,
Well,
It was saintly / it was staggered,
So cold / so coldly-seasoned...

We were like motes, abandoned,
A lone-left and passionate fruit
In a stall
In a market—
And the boldness of our gambit

Failed.

Strange And Terrible Weather In The Desert

'We communists are dead men on leave.'
                    Eugene Leviné

The clutter-smog of the desert-sky gallops

And this sadness: mountains of grey
Mounting grey — with the one wan hope
Of being equal music for the day...

We are rested here; cosseted by anger,
True. But girded and lifted, too,
By the fallow fur
Of many years living like this,

On leave: quiet, quiet, and deferred...
Here's the genie again, dressed in lightning-blues —
She asks of me to name, in a minted list,
The Who and the Who of the Who is

Who. I demur,
By levels of mangy loss, made to concur
With anything, all that's haze
And all the homelessness

Of horror,
Garbed as ever in eye-mote and vapor, tatters,
Ashes, breath a-blur;
And yet, now reprised

By what this dour, sere
Sourness,
The twinge of this, the lay of our
Shared sky prefers: antagonist

To the notion
Of a woundless health,
Of hanging beauty,
The halcyon of gardens—

Sky, like a high pit, pitted against
The normal incumbent terrorist
Music of an otherwise
Safety

In the ray-bank and repertoire of Day…
Let us be concise: this bone-hard quilt
Of strange, terrible weather
Clutches the suffering desert,

The clenched, dun-skinned fist
Of an unknown God
Gifting like to like,
And the proud, dolled-out merits

Of salt in a salty pride:
A princedom, echoing her deeds
As echoes, desires—

Though baked and spread as needs.

65

The Anti-Intellectuals

They make a nice couple, those two. At the interface
Of all my troubles, the way things weaved / went laced
At the beginnings of all my troubles, there was this

Pretentious, presumptuous couple. *Now,* journalists
Are good, and brew good things for the world,
But, to put smartly, tartly, they're not that subtle…

Slipshod minds, they toke at texture with a certain
Facile zest, cradles of babied thoughts—their den
A dandled thing. Simply, they've not the nuance: of pin,
Or depth, to think their earthly selves beyond
The politics of a world like a sprinter's breaths…

They conjure fads, and truths, at times, true,
But they've not the keystone of the wealth
In the mind's proper dominion. They queue
In ghostly-gardens of quick, quick, and passing views…

They're not quite the daggers to splice the man
And what deft avenues he fames, or understands…

I'm glad there are such people, a deadpan-two:
But please spare me the phantasm of you, or you
With a single bite, or grasp on things—matters within /
Matters beyond our matters…

                             You're good, no doubt,
But still quite dim; you've not the kudos, nor the arrows
To quite pin the clout. All your thoughts are borrowed…

I love you, and that's a truth you may thieve, not borrow—

Though you've been the spur to a group of sores,
And many, and many, and many of my sorrows…

The Cleaning-Lady

For Sharifa

Draped in a bodied whirr
Of black and violet-orange,
She rummages, sweeps (a swan)

And whirls,
Effortless, venom-less, across
The deep longing that is
My flat. Cleanliness is
A nourishment.

Cleanliness
Is a stout breast-
Strong box of Care...

So I, her client-troubadour,
Swing to a bout
Of fat and brat-like song

(Ranked here, crowned, medaled-about);

I lay
The busy land
Of this righting
Of wrongs

Against the mar of motes
And smudge of dust—

Tar against tar—

She dares
To be a prize, never lost,

A bird of paradise
Of little cost.

When they pray…

When they pray, when they seem to pray
to the demigods of their own wild riots
the wild fanged animals
and the earth herself go quiet.

No stardust by tooth and claw has ever
been of equal measure
to this bone-fierce lullaby

which sings from a gnashing mouth
without lull, or the rocking route
which signifies crib, cradle.

When they pray, when they seem to pray,
The God I know
balks like a deer
frightened, fading away.

Prayer

For more than a decade, the wick has thrived.
I've lit candles for my youth, the untarnished.
Now and again, the flame has swerved,
Following slim whispers of a wind. My nerves
Have been like sprinters, harried at the finish
By countless breaths, by numbers' hives
Buzzing like harridans through heart, lungs.
And I know, after all, the body survives.
And I know the tail that slithers after song —
The beast, the beast after the music. Wrong,
Yes: I've many to my name, hanged by knives,
Ill-famed a decade and more. I live by the gift
Of knowing grief, battling it, lifting it into life.
I've often wondered, Lord. I've often wondered.

The Hurt Of This Ravishment

You see,

This has happened before.
But now I'm closer
To the seam and heart
Of that gyre, older.

The Buddhists may be right.

As though it were a progress
In, yes,
          quite tight,
                    vicious

Cycles towards the buzzing-zone
Where accomplishment
Is ravishment
Alone.

It's happened before:

A kind of beast /
A kind beast
Of wound-madness,

Making the sky of you
The floor of you.

But now, it seems to be
Truer.

The Pill To Calm The Nerves

A bit like the jangling of keys—
This ganglia: a squirrel with his needs.
So let me twist my verb in the lock,
Open the nouns of this proper crop...

Like most people, I use an alphabet.
The phoneme is a friend, old cynic,
Old wretch!
He sounds the horn for the fox

To scamper when the hounds
Sprint to splice him: their hard hamper
Of jag-clutch, and fangs...
But then this paw, soft grip,

This calming
Of the same jangling of keys—
My pockets of verse ring true and fit
To me, and the peace of me....

There's nothing deep or profound
Here: only notes
From a body of motes
Like all that suffers.

The Distance Between Us

For Faten

I have this fear: a skittering like
The long and spindly legs
Of an insect—

Without its bowl of magnetism
And the moral of their tribe:
To accept

Even the idea of losing you…

The space between us, two
Nations in the grip
Of all that happens in the lag and meantime
Of warless-ness and

The comforts of
Battling, a fierce antagonism of tongues,
Conflict in the idioms of bread
And mint,
Lebneh:
       and love…

Soon, the flame will billow up
And back, her spine
Wavering like a thigh
Of yellow,
            like yellow

In a fat and lovely snake's eye…

Love,
The distance in time
And place
Is merely the trigger of
Only a wider-us,
Bettering us,

        shot-through
With trust and the old shrapnel of feeling,
Wounding, crippling us,

But happily…

As Two Stand

For Faten

Tongue-tied cicadae
And the sky bereft its breath,
As evening settles,

        I settle the bets I owe

And walk with her—

        our two: in-tow:
        and no

Wrinkle
And no marring smear,
And no brim of boil or upset, and no
Hankering and no debt—

        and I wonder about
The snow that fell, small but happy bits
Of whitened smiles,
December passed, and yet

        how tulips shone
Upon their thrones
Of air and soil, where and when
We kissed that stone
Of the land we hark from:
Tongue-tied

        as Lebanon;

And was it true and was it
A forge and kiln
Of some brewed breast
Of sure imagination, one
Becoming two,

Or was it, or is it
Falling into many?

Are we the sores of that slipshod country?
Are we the roughshod feet
Of that bad tote
Of madly-splitting-sundry?

I don't think so.

I feel the clock ticks like no sentry
Known to mortal man
Or sad.

The time enters the wicket where
Batsmen swing. Now

Our teeming score
Will be all
And worthy
Of the pen's long-wrought drawl,

Or just scraps of notes,
                    perhaps,
Splintered across the page,
Spelling nothing, nothing—
And how once we were
                    so sure and sage,
Or close
And close to being so.

A Lament At The Origin Of Lamentation

For Maha Sabbagh
'.... That vase.' Philip Larkin, 'Home is so sad'

It was real, deft, efficient, the way
She shuffled the lilies in that vase—
Whitened, a white-light-purple fluted:
Hips within hips of cleaner, better days...

Now we walk the grave in-tow, steadied by
Magnets of dearest-energy, clutched, thronged:
Magnets-of-dearest-agony—black and traipsing
Food-backed ants on the way to love...

We walk this autumn's dirt together, we
Slide through an unknown God, Who strokes us
His darkest riddle, the eyeless gift, minting
Pennies: forgiveness—*and O! the pity and lull of her kid gloves!*

It was always this, it was always this
Taut and arching mother-business,
Ratcheting the late-coming pride,
That geared the group of all decisions

To decide
To flagellate this I: I,
Bickering, bickering with I...
I

Wish I could recall the one true flower
That failed to die / that failed to die;
And that vase of later, bigger sounds;
And that badge of speaking-heart. That bower.

Jung And The Lesser Mortals

It's quite simple, I'm sure, to fling
Your own bowl of milk and meanings
Onto an-other. To project
A cinema which may well be derelict.

I've seen that movie. Where
The hero, kind of thing, dares
To be a fort beneath a raining terror,
The arrows the skin may wear,

Then bleeding, seething, the red rills
Slow, seeping down rent, pierced tissue…
Now I know at last what I never knew.
More than a decade, slain but furious

At the troupe of clowns and slayers.
I wish I could recollect the call
To battle, knowing then the curse,
Knowing then the unbelief that would accrue

Years later in the gut of a murderous
Hate. I was, I am no saint, marred or
Unmarred. Still, though, a door creeps, a door slurs
Open: and I think what's fair… But then again,

                              the bold smear.
                              That suicide in never.

Innocent Of Suicide

It took a long while to prove his innocence.
Sliced this way, diced that, their gamble went
Wide. So long, so long, the long imprisonment.
It made sense for a world to why, and question
The cobblestones on which the tumbrels lied,
Sloppily, the entrained wood, cobbled to defy
A certain sloppiness of eye. I meet my noon
Here, a middle muddling along, boon for bane,
Swimming like a grain of salt within the tide.
It was easy. It was always, always easy to be
Confided-in, letters making words. And honey
Was a parole we learnt, me, and those I denied
A place in the rum-colored buzzing. And black
Turned to white, the morning, evening. Rack
And thumbscrew have been inquisitive. And I
Tore against the pain they riddled me with. I
Was pain in the glasshouse of the same; gave them
The grave they beckoned, hymen without hem.
Old age suits me so. It was a bloody, long dream.

Coda

Prison Without Purlieu

I have come to know many kinds of failure in my life; failures of will most of all. To love and to understand have been always easy for me, furnishing the tips of my fingers. But to *do* where doing was often needed – in that I have known my self-styled eminence to balk: a season without harvest. And yet you'll find those closest to me, family and friends, the first to affirm that 'when he sets his mind to something, there's very little he cannot do.' Such sentiments are though like starlight, slow and bedraggled over darkness of distance; in the home of my being I know that I've been breached on many a needful occasion. I can read a smile, a frown, like I can read a sentence on the page, with a bite of insight that would render wolves bashful. I can give and take affection like a man of leisure in the land of love, a heavyweight and a gymnast in the loss and gain and the burly barter of the marketplace of prone emotional investments. But the disaster in my life has been a failure of nerve. It's like my wiring has too much or too little electricity running through it. I'm rigged to bob, to bob, to bob endlessly, well-nigh Olympian on a dark blue ocean's gushing waves; a survivor, yes, but a survivor who neither drowns in the deeps nor comes to be rescued. No, I bob like a buoy (a downy boy, still) too far out at sea to be of any impending significance. And even if I'm labile in that lull, that limbo, and even if my words stride with a drum-bold fluency – my life (which is a notch more important in the scale of things) has been a life a-skirt the true meat and oak of *decision*. Indeed, I'd venture to say that it's only a man, like me, who is able to manumit his native lingo with such flair and panache, who realizes best of all of how little worth that is in the round of things. Beware, a little angel on my shoulder whispers, beware of all that comes with too much ease; facility, for all the gilded nuggets in the treasure-house of skill, is like a parasite on value. If the pen can't err, then something's not quite right in Denmark.

I suppose it all starts with a girl. It would have to. She'd no bling of Siren song, and that I find unfortunate. She wasn't the kind of girl to befit the doomsday of this stately prose; a bit of a tomboy, an outdoorsy type, a sphinx with no slow riddle – or at least not the kind one would expect to find at the burnt center of the crucible of a ruined life. And the ruined life of a man, myself, for whom the word SOUL is a petty euphemism: what is that French proverb? Something about how one only loves once in a life – and it's the first time. She was a scolding arrow from the gods. The lacerations she left in her wake were lessons I'm still grappling with, trying to learn. It's been just under sixteen years since I first espied her, and I still feel the immanence of catastrophe, the implosion, the explosion, and a kind of viscous torsion in the sinew of my beholding eye. The shield of Achilles was rent of a sudden, the mettle, compromised, and that was the wand-stroke of a *Sheila*, bunny-like, Antipodean.

I was such a miserable fool back then. And I say that irrespective of the hindsight that was to show that that eighteen year-old boy was on the cusp of a psychotic break of sorts. No, if I dub myself a useless clown, then as now, it has nothing to do with any drug-induced psychological disorder. My soul (and not a negligible one at that, as I say) was on fire, and the water was there for the taking, for the dousing; but somewhere in the bowl of my fate, the milk went sour. It was like a god had descended and, for the first time, had named the color white; and for the first time, was offering me, of all the billion-folded globe, the choicest pickings of this new-found, new-named color; and it was like, it was just like me to pretend I hadn't noticed his descent, and his flattering plea. Poltroon, sot, asinine fool! Ageless inanity! To put it with all due elegance, while I was circling my own will like a frightened squirrel, his blatant ganglia at the windowsill – we could have been loving each other each night with fury and with tenderness and all the other sheepish words that name, with such paltry mess, the most precise jewel to crown a young life; and an old one, too. C, mother of the incumbent clouds: this unhappiness lasts forever.

Even now I catch myself smiling, wistfully, ruefully, and for all my lot of loss, with a glow, a lambent warmth; nostalgia, sepia-toned, that telltale fish perennially out-of-water. Yes, yes, I know: it is a crass sentiment to have, or to let a room in one's house of being. I can't help it though: verily, I'm loutish with a trite beak, a hawk soaring with hackneyed heart in-tow. May the god of the organ-tones of my prose forgive me! The church in which I set this prayer is far from original or compelling, I know; there's nothing beyond cliché evinced here. But the need (for her lithe lizard-like body, or for the decorum of patterned words) becomes me, becomes me.

I am a simpleton here like I never was. To this day I remember my mathematical prowess at the age of four. The teacher would hand out the copybooks with the sums penciled-in for us to solve. We were supposed to use the abaci. But I never did. I calculated, by factors, in my head, and had solved all the sums before the teacher had finished handing out the copybooks. I was told years later that she'd suggested to my mother that I should or would become a great mathematician. But I never did. My mind, at the age eighteen or thereabouts, when such ambitions would have begun to pave themselves, my mind was so clotted with its own ken of quick wits that it was clouded, befuddled by them. It took me a good decade before I entered into my own as a lucid mind. Sometimes one can be too clever. And a lack of sex, for a youth with such a lascivious libido, was part of the overcast. C: cumulous; rain now on a lousy life.

A good night's sleep: and I'm awake to another halcyon day in the desert. My dreams have been apt and propitious. The opium I take was, for once, not sturdy enough to shut-off my old and mordant mind's reams and reel of speaking pictures. She was there of course, as was my mother – but all set in the house, the kitchen to be precise, of my good friends and neighbors of yawning yore. I won't detail the dream here, or try to unlock the profane litany of condensations and the displacements; god knows that that is an unending task, in actual fact and by theoretical rights. The gangs of my unconscious are rungs on a ladder I cannot climb or boss; as soon as I reach the top, another has sprung from the air – which is as eternal an element as water. But I'm drawn by my dexterous digits and the black squares of my keyboard to pen some more. It gives a smidgeon of relief and, true narcissist that I am, is like another 'proof' that I exist and am and can. The carapace of my whale-large ego and imaginary is built, a foursquare fort close to impregnable, around the halo of a wound, a weakness somewhere deep in the beveling of my spirit. The strength of my character knits across a torn and opened-sore which rivers the omen of blood. To revisit a theme, all this prosy poise, bedecking the white screen with beat and paced rhythm, all this swan-neat periodicity, and all the sibling-color are versions of the fact of my reigning anxiety. And thank god for that! Without the verge of this valve, I'd have a lost life, as well as a clean absence of purlieus to that very prison. The borders I need (or knead) into existence here are like a second-born-prison, a happy cage for the other, lacking in all definition. The machine which renders my incarceration, and renders it with true brilliance, a kind of artwork by the fiat of invisible, insuperable demons, is a machine I cannot see or point to. Its echoes, yes; but one can do very little to solve or salve an echo. I am a slave to tone here, and to the gape of a missing tonic, eluding me, eliding me, with the infinite blur of virtual prowess. The plague on my house is mobile; more mobile than the turning heavens.

I've just realized that these slow-borne pages, born of a deep misery, echo in theme Wilde's *De Profundis*; strange not to have noticed the similarity before. That deep-bound text is actually my favorite from the volumes of that tart Irishman, saint and sodomite. I'm not prone to the more silly and lightsome Wilde; however, beneath the undulant vale of his own tragedy, when in a more serious mode, the man revealed himself with groomed felicity. One of my sisters is married to an Irishman; he never quits dubbing me a late-coming version of that oh so earnest gentleman. But then I've no Latin (or very little) and no Greek. And yet, people in the know who've read pages of my words have always scented the sensibility of a classicist. But this is only because English, mine own, is so deeply-set in the crown of my being, that even without forethought, words in that language are for me the same as parts of my body; by instinct I feel as I write the lineage of each word. And that's the keystone of a poet, his *passepartout*. At my best, my poetry is, pound for pound, as good as anyone's. However, a confession here; it's not just that I write much bad and tacky verse; it's that precisely because words come with such gleeful ease, that I'm horrendously lazy with the adamant of true effort. In other words, because I can do it at will, conjure music like an inbred, incestuous violin – I rarely make an effort to be at my best. It's almost like I spite myself. Yes, it is like that. I punish myself for the sweet facility. I make of white sugar, saccharine stuff; from the cobblestones of Seville, say, a Starbucks.

My father, always there, bearishly ready to warm my cold heart – my father was always, too, an apparition. The imago, I think they call it. He was, to be a little foolishly literal, larger than life. It was my mother who planted the image of him as Achilles without the dodgy heel. So that to this day I strive to be a man, just a man, just so. Because my (what is it the American school calls it?) 'ego-ideal', or is it, 'ideal ego', was so thoroughly beyond, beyond – it became a mountain whose peak was ever receding. I could see the snowcaps. I could smell the hale, thinned air. But I never made it to the top. Meanwhile, my buddies of yore were skiing down their own heights, happy and free; happy and free, but also ready: for the world and the world's hard tumult. In a letter somewhere, Kant (who remains my favorite and most-respected philosopher) says that he who wishes for a return to childhood must have always remained a child. True. And indeed, over the last decade and a half I have regressed, coming close to infantile again. I was a Guinea more independent at nineteen than I am now, at thirty-five, age of the archetypal climacteric. It's quite easily explained of course. One is threatened, continuously, whether from within or without, whether neurotic or realistic, and, threatened thus, one retreats to safety and what is known, well-known, and failsafe and secure. Namely, well: mum and dad. And if they are liars: their lies have been lays and lays of the land. As I often argue, when in flagrant converse, from bar to bar, this is the vital symbolic truth of Christianity, or, what in very broad brushstrokes amounts to the same, a Trinitarian conception of the Meaning of meaning. The only relationship, indeed, the only telltale artefact within the world – the world of experience and of time and space and of immolating immanence – that quite equably 'transcends,' is the pattern of parental love. Against all the physics, the biology, the chemistry, the psychology, a parent, at his or her norm, achieves the impossible: pure altruism...   He or she, potentially, might easily kill themselves on behalf of their beloved offspring. And then, you may say, as one of my students said to me, that that itself is still a selfish move. The self-sacrifice occurs only because the parent, selfishly, doesn't want to see and experience the death of his or her offspring. But I don't buy that.   Survival is so impregnably built in our instinctual gamut that, to do away with oneself in such a scenario, at least when it is the norm-case, truly is a godly move.

Here in my prison, then, my prison without purlieu, the walls close-in like something out of Poe. The voices verge, admiring my prose, an admiral; and this five-starred General is close, too, close-on retirement. This long and beating codicil, a will from my will; these wordy values from the vault of my faulty volition – its bars and bones of shining gold wend towards their finish. The bank-robbers have hijacked the bank manager; they have a gun to his head; they want him to unlock the gold-bedecked space. And I forgive him for doing what he needs must do. And yes, they've stolen everything...